JAZZSTEPS 2
Putting it Together

Further jazz improvising for beginners

by Graham Robb

Contents

Additional parts available through Faberprint, 3 Queen Square, London WC1N 3AU

© 1993 by Faber Music Ltd
First published by Faber Music Ltd
3 Queen Square London WC1N 3AU
Cover design by Lynette Williamson
Music set by Silverfen
Printed in England by Caligraving Ltd
All rights reserved

ISBN 0 571 51369 7

FABER *ff* MUSIC

How to Put it Together . . .

Jazzsteps is an aural-based, step by step improvising method. The complete package consists of the play-along tape and this book, and in order to get the most out of this way of learning you will need both. It is organised so that you can use and then 're-use' the tape and book as new ideas are introduced.

Putting it Together, which follows on from the first Jazzsteps book, **Starting Out**, is designed to help all musicians – whether beginners or more experienced players – to improvise jazz. Don't worry if you haven't worked through **Starting Out** – if you can already play simple, short improvised phrases, but want to go further, then you are ready for **Putting it Together**.

The tape After a quick recap of Jazzsteps 1 to 5 (explained more fully in **Starting Out**), Side A of the tape guides you through Jazzstep 6, explaining what you do at each stage. Side B of the tape contains four *Play-along Pieces*, designed to enable you to consolidate what you have learnt on Side A. It goes on to explain Jazzsteps 7, 8, 9, 10 and 11 – each demonstrating new ways of using *A-Section Grooves* (from Side A) and the Play-along Pieces. The 'Contents Clock' is a graphic view of what the tape contains – each side is 30 minutes long, and you can therefore see at a glance the length of time occupied by each section.

The book The book complements the tape, providing detailed explanation of each Jazzstep, the tune *Bouncing Buddies*, and further musical notation for instruments in C, B♭ and E♭, and bass instruments, including the four *Play-along Pieces*. The italic text in the left margin of each page summarizes the tape contents. You will find it easier to read the relevant section immediately before working with the tape rather than trying to absorb everything before you start. The Teacher Notes at the back explain how **Jazzsteps** can be used in a group context, and offer advice on assessment.

Hints and tips

The following suggestions are intended to help you get the most out of **Putting it Together**.

1 The first time you use the tape, zero the tape counter at the start of side A and as you reach each new section, fill in the tape location boxes on the 'Contents Clock' (page 3). Do the same for Side B, remembering to zero the counter before you start.

2 Try to practise every day: little and often is better than an occasional marathon session.

3 Be sure that you understand each section and you are confident with your playing before moving on: try to avoid rushing on to the next section before you are ready; equally, try to avoid getting stuck.

4 Many musicians find it difficult to overcome shyness when asked to

sing, but singing your original phrases as a preliminary to playing them on your instrument will help to develop musical confidence.

5 Singers and drummers can use **Putting it Together** in exactly the same way as other instrumentalists. Singers: instead of singing the notes to *la-la-la*, try using syllables like *bee-ba-doo-dap* – you will find it easier to swing. Drummers: work through the note-learning sections at least once, improvising your part on the full kit. Make sure you are phrasing exactly with the tune. When playing the groove games, *start* on the snare drum only, moving on to the full kit as ideas develop.

6 Keyboard players may improvise a left-hand part using the chord symbols provided. If there is no bass player available, try incorporating the bass-line from the bass/drums part of the *Play-along Pieces* into the left-hand.

7 Make sure you can hear the tape *and* yourself clearly. If you are using headphones for instance, have one ear on and one ear off.

The tape 'Contents Clock'

(timings are approximate)

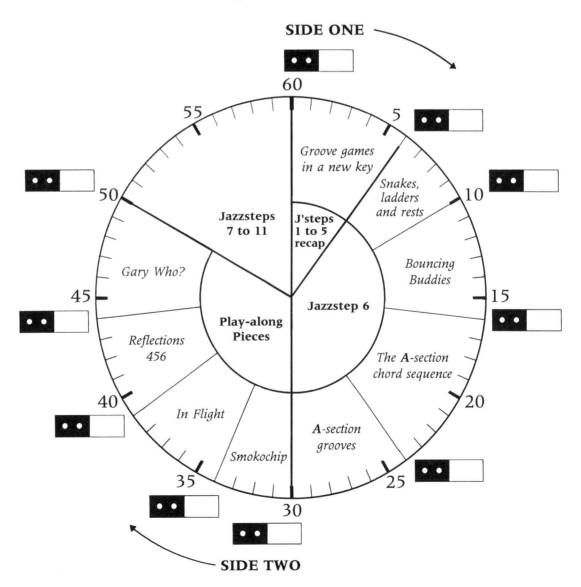

Groove games in a new key

(SIDE A) This is an opportunity to recap Jazzsteps 1 to 5, but playing in a new key. The Groove games are musical questions and answers: you will hear a short phrase played by the band to which you then respond.

*Jazzsteps 1 to 5 recap ***

Jazzstep 1 Rhythm groove games.

rhythm groove games demo After the two-bar count-in you will hear, over the rhythm section, some short phrases played on the piano and copied by the guitar.

your turn The rhythm section continues and after each piano phrase there is a gap: repeat each phrase exactly as you hear it on your instrument. The starting note is the root note of the chord: this is printed in the correct key for your instrument on page 12, 13, 14 or 15. If you like, you can try clapping the rhythms and then singing the phrases before you play them.

Jazzstep 2 Singing groove games

singing groove games Rewind the tape to the Jazzstep 1 groove games, but this time, instead of repeating the given phrases, *sing* your own improvised answering phrases. Start each phrase on the same first note as the given phrase but continue with whatever comes into your head to make a short phrase of about the same length – you will find it easier to 'swing' if you use phrases like *bee-ba-doo-dap* rather than *la-la-la-la*! Try to keep your phrases as simple and 'jazzy' as you can.

Jazzstep 3 Now it's time to play your improvised answering phrases on your instrument. But first, you will need to know a little bit of music theory to help you decide which notes to play.

> *All the music you will play and improvise in* **Putting it Together** *is based on the mixolydian scale and chord on F, i.e. F7 (concert pitch).*
>
> *Reminder: The* **chord tones** *are the four notes which make up the basic seventh chord - the root, third, fifth and seventh. The* **scale tones** *are the notes of the scale which will fit, i.e. sound okay, played over that chord.*

mixolydian scale and dominant seventh chord demo The scale and chord tones are demonstrated on the tape and also written out in music notation in the correct key for your instrument (page 12, 13, 14 or 15). Listen to the scale and chord.

play scale and chord over click Play the mixolydian scale and the chord of the dominant seventh chord along with the tape.

improvise your own answering phrases Rewind the tape to the Jazzstep 1 groove games and try improvising your own answering phrases, using exactly the same rhythm as the given phrase. Remember to use only **scale tones** from the mixolydian scale and start and end your phrase on any **chord tone**.

* Jazzsteps 1 to 5 are covered more fully in **Starting Out**

Jazzstep 4   Work through the Jazzstep 1 groove games again, this time improvising the rhythm as well. Let your answering phrases follow the same melodic shape as the given phrase: concentrate on playing rhythmically and with a good 'swing' feel.

Jazzstep 5   With Jazzstep 5, you improvise a continuous jazz solo, by making up question and answer phrases and joining them all together. Jazzstep 6 and the rest of **Putting it Together** develop new ideas which will help you structure these more extended solos.

6 Jazzstep 6

Snakes, ladders and rests

Now you are ready to improvise your own original phrases. Snakes, ladders and rests are designed to help you focus your ideas:

Snakes, ladders and rests demo   Look at the music page for your instrument (page 12, 13, 14 or 15) and listen to the phrases played on the tape. Notice the shape of the snake phrases, which use stepwise scale tones, and ladder phrases, which use just the chord tones.

> *Phrases based on stepwise scale tones are* **snakes**.
> *Phrases based on chord tones are* **ladders**.
> **Rests** *in between each phrase give you time to think.*

your turn   Make up your own phrases using snakes, ladders and rests over the latin rhythm. Start by using snakes, up or down, playing for two bars and then resting for two bars. The rest bars allow you time to consider the phrase you have just played and think about the next one. Then try phrases using ladders too. You don't need to play a lot of notes – try to play rhythmic phrases with a good 'swing' feel. Jazzstep 1 – repeating your own 2-bar phrases – may help you to focus your ideas.

A new tune: Bouncing Buddies

Bouncing Buddies is in **AABA** form. This means that it starts with an **A** section, which is played twice; it is followed by a **B** section (different music); and then the **A** section is played again. In *Bouncing Buddies*, each section lasts for 8 bars, so the complete tune is 32 bars long. The **B** section is sometimes referred to as the 'middle eight' (i.e. the middle 8-bar section). Sometimes, the odd note or rhythm is varied in the repeats of the **A** section.

AABA is a very common form in jazz. It is a simple but effective way to structure the music, and will also be used later when you improvise jazz solos to four new pieces.

6

Bouncing Buddies demo	You'll find the tune printed in the correct key for your instrument on one of the following pages – 12, 13, 14 or 15. Don't worry if you can't read music very fluently as you'll quickly pick it up by ear. First of all just listen to the demo.
Bouncing Buddies your turn	The band will play the melody once, a little more slowly. Then you play it on your instrument while the band continues as an accompaniment.
slow *Bouncing Buddies*	Now an even slower version. Come in straight after the count-in and play along with the melody on the tape.
Bouncing Buddies up to speed	Listen to the melody once, now up to speed, then play the repeat.

Bouncing Buddies – the A-section chord sequence

Now you are ready to try improvising your own original phrases over the changing chord sequence in the **A** section of *Bouncing Buddies* – which is less complicated than it sounds, because the notes of the mixolydian scale will fit (i.e. sound okay) with **all** the chords in the sequence.

But first, read the following explanation of chords. You will find it printed in music notation in the correct key for your instrument on page 12, 13, 14 or 15 ('AABA' chord sequence).

> *The **A** section consists of a sequence of four chords – chord six, chord two, chord five and chord one – which are notated as roman numerals, like this: VI II V I.*
>
> *Each of these is a seventh chord, i.e. made up of the root, third, fifth and seventh. Thus the full notation is: VI7 II7 V7 Imaj7.*
>
> *Chords VI7 and II7 are minor seventh chords, while V7 is the dominant seventh chord you having been using for all your improvising so far. Chord Imaj7 is a major seventh chord i.e. 'sharpened seventh' and is therefore notated with the abbreviation 'maj'.*

A-*section chord sequence demo*	Listen to the demo and notice where the chords change.
play chord tones over backing	Turn to the music page for your instrument and play the chord tones along with the tape. You will play the sequence twice.
scale over chord sequence demo	Listen to how the mixolydian scale fits over the chord sequence.
play mixolydian scale over chord sequence	Play the scale over the chord sequence, again listening carefully to how the notes fit with each chord. You may notice that some scale tones clash with a chord, especially if it happens right on a chord change. The 'clash' is caused by playing a note which doesn't belong to the chord, but it will immediately be resolved when you play the next scale tone up or down. Experienced jazz improvisers purposely play these clashes to create tension and excitement in the music.
stepwise forced move demo	In this sequence of chords, any melody notes which are not chord tones will clash with the chord; they can be 'corrected' by moving up or down one note of the mixolydian scale. Listen to how easily clashes can be resolved.

ascending long scale tones over the chord sequence	Start on any note of the mixolydian scale. If it doesn't fit with the first chord, go up by step and the next note will. Stay on each note for as long as possible – at each chord change listen to whether the note you are playing fits with the new chord; if it clashes move up by step again. Use your ears to decide!
descending long scale tones over the chord sequence	Try the same again, this time start on a high note and go **down** by step to resolve the clashes.
slow jazz over chord sequence demo	Listen to the phrases: each new one starts on a chord tone.
play slow jazz over the chord sequence	Slowly negotiate the chord sequence by improvising short phrases of snakes, ladders and rests. Avoid bad clashes by playing a chord tone of the new chord as each one changes. If you want to have another go, rewind to the beginning of the **A-section chord sequence**.

A-section grooves

Now you are ready to improvise your own short, original phrases over different **A**-section grooves, up to speed. The 'groove' of a jazz piece is the 'feel'/style.

A-*section groove demo*	Listen to the demo of snakes, ladders and rests over the **A**-section chord sequence, up to speed.
A-*section groove - your turn*	Using the notes of the mixolydian scale, improvise your own short phrases of snakes, ladders and rests at the faster tempo. This is the same as you did in *Snakes, ladders and rests* at the start of Jazzstep 6, but now each phrase is over a different chord.
another **A**-*section groove*	This groove uses exactly the same chord sequence, but the chords change at a different rate. Listen carefully to make sure your hear the changes.
***Bouncing Buddies** arrangement*	*Bouncing Buddies* uses these four chords in its **A** section. Play the tune, as printed, at the beginning and end of the arrangement. In between, in the jazz solo section, improvise short phrases over the chords. A drum fill will tell you when to play the tune for the last time.
(end of SIDE A)	

Play-along Pieces

(SIDE B)	There are four Play-along Pieces and you will find the music in the correct key for your instrument in one of the separate parts with this book.

Smokochip is in a synthy-sounding jazz/rock style.

In Flight is a piano trio jazz waltz.

Reflections 456 is a piano ballad.

Gary Who? is in a 'straight ahead' jazz style, featuring vibraphone.

Each piece is in **AABA** form. A complete **AABA** sequence is usually referred to as a **chorus**; thus each piece is made up of many choruses i.e. many repeats of the complete **AABA** structure. In the first and last choruses you will play the tune as printed. In between is the jazz solo section where you will improvise over the chords; when playing 'live' this may consist of as many choruses as you like.

The **A** sections of each of these four Play-along Pieces have exactly the same chord sequence as the *Bouncing Buddies* **A** section – VI7 II7 V7 Imaj7. The **B** sections (middle 8) of each piece are all different, and for now simply rest and listen for eight bars as they occur.

If you like, start by just listening to each piece, following each **AABA** chorus and the chord sequence of the **A** section in the printed arrangement. To help you keep your place, there are drum fills into and out of each **B** section and at the start of the last chorus. Then have a go at the complete arrangement yourself. In the jazz solo section, remember to keep your original phrases short, with rests in between each phrase. The drum fill will remind you when to play the tune for the last chorus.

7 Jazzstep 7

Now you are ready to improvise a longer, four-bar phrase by combining Jazzstep 6 and Jazzstep 3: improvise your own, original two-bar phrase as you have been practising, and immediately answer it with another two-bar phrase which has exactly the same rhythm. Use the notes of the mixolydian scale for both phrases but each time your first phrase will be over chord VI7 and your answering phrase over chord II7. Rest for four bars between each pair of phrases.

demo Listen to the demo.

your turn Rewind the tape to **A-section grooves** on Side A and work through the grooves, improvising four-bar phrases over chords VI7 and II7 and then resting for four bars. Continue in the same way with the Play-along Pieces, but improvise in the **A** sections only; rest and listen to the middle 8 (**B** section) each time it occurs.

8 Jazzstep 8

This is a combination of Jazzstep 6 and Jazzstep 4: improvise your own, original two-bar phrase as before, but this time immediately answer it with a two-bar phrase which has a different rhythm but follows the same melodic shape as your first phrase. Have fun with the rhythms. Use the notes of the mixolydian scales and remember that your first phrase will be over chord VI7 and your answering phrase over chord II7. Rest for four bars between each pair of phrases.

demo Listen to the demo.

your turn Rewind the tape to **A-section grooves** on Side A and work through each groove. Continue with the Play-along Pieces, but remember to rest and listen to the middle 8 each time it occurs.

9 Jazzstep 9

With this jazzstep, you will decide before playing how to shape the phrases i.e. whether the phrases will go up, down or start and end on the same note.

ascending phrases demo Listen to the demo: notice how the phrases climb so that the last note of each phrase is higher than the first note.

ascending phrases - your turn Rewind the tape to **A-section grooves** and work through the grooves, making sure that each phrase ends on a chord tone higher than the one it started on. Continue in the same way with the Play-along Pieces, but remember to rest and listen to the middle 8 each time it occurs.

descending phrases Work through the **A-section grooves** and Play-along Pieces again, this time making sure that each phrase ends on a chord tone *lower* than the one on which it started.

start and end on same note Finally, work through **A-section grooves** and the Play-along Pieces, playing phrases that start and end on the same note.

rest and play demo So far in Jazzsteps 7, 8 and 9, you have been improvising for the first four bars of the **A** section, over chords VI7 and II7, and then resting for four bars. Now listen to a demo of this the other way around: resting for four bars and then improvising for four bars over chords V7 and Imaj7. If you need to refresh your memory about these two chords, rewind the tape to **The A-section chord sequence** on Side A.

rest and play - your turn Work through **A-section grooves**: start each jazz solo section by resting for four bars and then improvise phrases over chords V7 and Imaj7. Continue in the same way with the Play-along Pieces, but still just rest and listen to the **B** sections. For your improvisations, use a mixture of ideas from Jazzsteps 7, 8 and 9.

The B section (the 'middle 8')

So far, you have been improvising in just the **A** section of each piece – now it's time to look at the **B** section, or 'middle 8'. Turn to the music page for your instrument and look at the **B** section of *Bouncing Buddies*; although there are two new chords, the notes of the mixolydian scale will still fit.

Bouncing Buddies middle 8 demo Follow the chord sequence as printed.

play chord tones Play the chord tones along with the band on the tape.

scale over chords demo Listen to how the mixolydian scale fits over the chords.

| play mixolydian scale over chords | Play the mixolydian scale over the chords. |

Bouncing Buddies: *complete sequence* — Play the tune as printed at the beginning and end of the arrangement. In between, in the jazz solo section, improvise your own short phrases using Jazzsteps 7, 8 and 9 over the complete **AABA** sequence. To help you keep your place, there are drum fills into and out of each middle 8 and at the start of the last chorus, when you will play the tune again.

Play-along Pieces: complete sequence — In the Play-along Pieces, the middle 8 chord symbols and chord tones are printed within the arrangement. The mixolydian scale fits over them all. To begin with, you might like to play just the chord tones or the mixolydian scale each time the middle 8 section occurs. When you are more familiar with the chords, try Jazzsteps 7, 8 and 9 over the complete **AABA** sequence.

10 Jazzstep 10

In Jazzstep 10, your jazz solos become more continuous: join together two pairs of phrases so that you play for eight bars and then rest for four bars.

Jazzstep 10 demo — Listen to the demo. Notice how the phrases stop and start half-way through **A** and **B** sections.

Jazzstep 10 - your turn — You may find it difficult to keep your place in the sequence as you find yourself starting and ending eight-bar phrases in the middle of **A** and **B** sections. To start with, you may find it easier to count bars, but try to listen to the rhythm section at the same time. With practice, it becomes easier to *feel* where you are. Start with **A-section grooves** (**A**-section chords only), then continue with the Play-along Pieces, improvising over the complete **AABA** sequence.

11 Jazzstep 11

This jazzstep is similar to Jazzstep 5 in *Starting Out*, but instead of just shutting your eyes and going for it, think about the *length* of your phrases. Play phrases of odd lengths, stopping and starting in the middle of **A** or **B** sections, and use the rests in between to consider the phrase you have just played and to plan the next one.

Jazzstep 11 demo — Listen to how the length of each phrase is **not** dictated by the **AABA** structure. The fact that the phrases are all of odd lengths helps to make the solos more interesting straight away.

Jazzstep 11 - your turn — Rewind the tape to **A-section grooves** and have a go at Jazzstep 11. Continue with all the Play-along Pieces.

As well as practising all the jazzsteps and thinking carefully about how to structure each phrase, occasionally allow yourself to play through the Play-along Pieces *without* thinking too hard. Let yourself 'just play' – it's very easy to lose sight of how much fun jazz improvisation can be – so from time to time give yourself a chance to just enjoy it!

Jazzsteps Live!

Using the written out arrangements of the Play-along Pieces as a guide, have a go at performing as a group of players – using any available instruments – without the tape backing. Ideally, you need at least one bass instrument or keyboard to play the independent bass line in the Bass/Drums/Percussion part. If you have a drummer, use the given drum rhythm(s), with variations *ad lib*, throughout your performance. Chordal backing may be provided by a guitarist or keyboard player using the chord symbols as a guide. Melody instruments can then solo over this backing, repeating the jazz solo sections many times so that everyone has a go. To begin and end your performance, play the tune as written twice at the beginning, and twice at the end.

With practice, you will soon be well on the way to creating convincing jazz improvisations with understanding and confidence. But remember to keep it simple and take one **Jazzstep** at a time!

Jazzsteps Summary

Jazzstep 1	repeating a given phrase exactly as you hear it.
Jazzstep 2	singing an improvised answering phrase to a given phrase.
Jazzstep 3	playing an improvised answer using the same rhythm as the given phrase.
Jazzstep 4	playing an improvised answer with your own rhythms.
Jazzstep 5	improvising both question and answer to form a continuous jazz solo section.
Jazzstep 6	*Snakes, ladders and rests* – developing new ideas to improvise short original phrases.
Jazzstep 7	combination of Jazzsteps 6 and 3 – improvising 4-bar phrases by playing an original 2-bar phrase and answering it with another 2-bar phrase using exactly the same rhythm.
Jazzstep 8	combination of Jazzsteps 6 and 4 – improvising 4-bar phrases by playing an original 2-bar phrase and answering it with another 2-bar phrase using a different rhythm.
Jazzstep 9	improvising 4-bar phrases, but deciding on the melodic shape of the phrases before you start.
Jazzstep 10	improvising for 8-bars, resting for 4.
Jazzstep 11	freely improvising jazz solos using phrases of varying lengths.

Piano/Keyboard/
Guitar/Flute/Violin/
Recorder/Oboe

Music Page

for C instruments

Mixolydian scale tones on F (F7)

Mixolydian chord tones on F (F7)

root   third   fifth   seventh

Snakes, ladders and rests

snake   *rest*   *snake*   *ladder*   *rest*

ladder   *rest*   *mixture (mostly snake)*

Bouncing Buddies

Gm7   Cm7   F7

1st time   2nd time   *Fine (last time)*   Bbmaj7   Ebmaj7

Bbmaj7   Bbmaj7

Dm7   Cm7   F7   *D.C. al Fine*

AABA chord sequence

A section

Gm7   Cm7   F7   Bbmaj7

B section

Ebmaj7   Dm7   Cm7   F7   *play* **A** *once again*

Clarinet/Trumpet/Tenor saxophone/
Soprano saxophone/Flugelhorn

Music Page
for Bb instruments

Alto/Baritone saxophone

Music Page

for E♭ instruments

Mixolydian scale tones on D (D7)

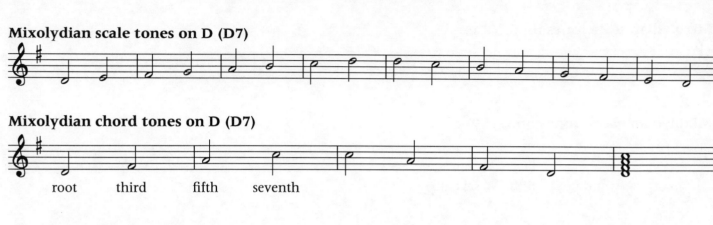

Mixolydian chord tones on D (D7)

root   third   fifth   seventh

Snakes, ladders and rests

snake   *rest*   *snake*   *ladder*   *rest*

ladder   *rest*   *mixture (mostly snake)*

Bouncing Buddies

A Em7   Am7   D7

1st time
Gmaj7   2nd time
Gmaj7   *Fine (last time)*   B Cmaj7

Bm7   Am7   D7   *D.C. al Fine*

AABA chord sequence

A section

Em7   Am7   D7   Gmaj7

B section   *play* A *once again*

Cmaj7   Bm7   Am7   D7

Bass guitar/Double bass/
Trombone/Tuba/Cello/Bassoon/

Music Page

for bass instruments

Mixolydian scale tones on F (F7)

Mixolydian chord tones on F (F7)

root   third   fifth   seventh

Snakes, ladders and rests

Bouncing Buddies

AABA chord sequence

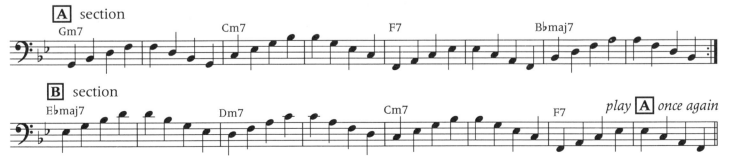

Teacher Notes

The section **How to Put it Together . . .** (page 2) applies equally in more formal educational situations. Class and instrumental teachers (who do not need to be experienced jazz musicians) may use this package very successfully as the basis for both group-work and special projects.

Putting it Together can be used with large music classes in several ways. *Groove Games in a New Key* is a quick recap of Jazzsteps 1 to 4 from **Starting Out** and the pupils can repeat the phrases in unison, but should improvise individually. In Jazzstep 6, individuals improvise their own original phrases and later – in Jazzsteps 7 and 8 – improvise answering phrases. In Jazzstep 9, pairs of pupils may alternate four bar phrases and in Jazzsteps 10 and 11, they could try alternating whole choruses.

The class may also be split into smaller groups, either by instrument or by ability, each group working with their own copy of the tape. With only a minimum of supervision, such groups, or even individual pupils, should be more-or-less self-sufficient with the material.

Assessment

Putting it Together is the second stage of a course which has two main purposes: to encourage the musician to attempt improvisation for the first time; and then to go on to improve on this established basic level. For this reason it is much better that improvisation happens at all than that it is scrutinised in minute detail and judged to be right or wrong.

The material is structured to give ample opportunity for both continuous and formative assessment. The Jazzsteps 1 to 4 recap, Jazzstep 6 and the four Play-along Pieces may be used as landmarks for lesson planning and assessment. Jazzsteps 7 to 11 re-use most of the material, and again can be used to structure both teaching and assessment.

In some ways, the task that you will be setting your pupils is not difficult; all they have to do is make up some short phrases, choosing from a limited number of notes, and play them in time to an accompaniment. Obviously, this becomes more difficult when the phrases are joined to make longer solos, but the most important skill is the ability to improvise convincingly and with the necessary panache. In this context, the pupil's playing must combine a good rhythmic sense with some degree of individuality. It must also be well integrated with the accompaniment. This integration will only happen if the players listen closely to the accompaniment and remain relaxed as they play.

Rhythmic playing, as opposed to rhythmically complex playing, is much more important than the choice of notes – which is deliberately restricted to the scale and chord tones of a single mixolydian mode. Attention can then be focused on the jazz 'feel' of the music. It must swing!

In the initial stages, instrumental or vocal technique is secondary to the musical content of the improvisation. Pupils will tend to play things that they find easy, as indeed do professional improvisers. If your pupils find improvisation enjoyable, and most do, those with a limited technique may well become motivated to improve.

Like **Starting Out**, **Putting it Together** is not intended to take the place of more conventional instrumental teaching and learning, and is best used as part of an integrated course in which all facets of music education are represented.